THE 100 BEST
SWIMMING POOLS

BETA-PLUS

THE 100 BEST
SWIMMING POOLS

CONTENTS

THE OUTDOOR SWIMMING POOL
OF A DIRECTOIRE HOUSE

Architect Bernard De Clerck has lived in this early-nineteenth-century Directoire house for around ten years. The house has been restored with respect for the spirit of the Directoire style: pure, not too much ornamentation, with sensible proportions and a light and airy atmosphere. An orangery was added to the property, and an outdoor swimming pool.

info@bernarddeclerck.be

The leaves of the magnolia filter the bright sunlight.

This central grass path bordered by old box gives structure to the garden.

PROTECTED FROM THE MISTRAL

This swimming pool is situated in the immediate surroundings of Aix-en-Provence.
The pool is on a lower level, protected from the mistral.
The loungers with white cushions are from Gandia Blasco,
model Na Xamena (a Ramon Esteve design).

BESIDE THE BAY OF SAINT-TROPEZ

This villa beside the bay of Saint-Tropez was designed in 1950 by architect
Raymond Louis and beautifully renovated by architect Michel Lesot and
interior designer Gilles de Meulemeester (Ebony Interiors).
The large teakwood terraces and the swimming pool provide
a constantly changing view of the bay.

AN UNDERSTATED HOLIDAY HOME IN RAMATUELLE

Christel De Vos (De Vos Projects) created this newly built villa in Ramatuelle, in collaboration with Nathalie Mousny. The house was given a stucco finish and painted white; only the roof tiles reveal a Provençal inspiration. Antheunis supplied the swimming pool equipment and the Bisazza glass mosaic for the lining. The white garden chairs and table are by Tribu. The stone was found in a local quarry.

christeldevos1@gmail.com

A MODERN RESIDENTIAL BLOCK
WITH A BREATHTAKING SEA VIEW

Collection Privée is a renowned interior-design store with branches in Cannes and Valbonne. The company also has a studio for architecture and interior design, headed by Gilles Pellerin and Nicolette Schouten. The project in this report is the architectural studio's most recent creation on the Côte d'Azur: a defiantly contemporary variant on the Provençal villa. Geometric shapes, symmetry and balance are the key to this simply designed block. Teakwood was chosen for around the swimming pool. The infinity swimming pool is in stone mosaic tiles.

www.collection-privee.com

CONTEMPORARY AXES AND PERSPECTIVES IN THE MASSIF DES MAURES

Architect Marc Lust did not restrict himself to simply designing this project. He also put his own work on the backburner for three years to carry out the project himself. This property, situated in the Massif des Maures, between Hyères and Fréjus, is a perfect expression of his outlook on contemporary architecture. This is characterised by a clearly defined network of axes and perspectives and by the use of light as a fundamental element in the creation of a streamlined and chic space.

www.anthracite-st-tropez.com

The terrace area, distributed over different levels, connects the house to the swimming pool. The pool house – with a sun terrace and covered barbecue area – complements the design of the space surrounding the swimming pool. The use of natural stone, teak and white pebbles clearly delineates the entrance and relaxation zones. Stretched tent-cloth provides shade and lends a light-hearted touch.

The elongated form of the swimming pool (20 x 4 metres), an extension of the axis leading to the main entrance, emphasises the lines of the building and its impact on the surrounding nature. The existing Mediterranean vegetation, trimmed into spheres, creates the impression that the architectural project has not imposed itself, but that the natural environment has incorporated it.

AS THOUGH RISEN FROM THE ASHES

The Brabant farm in this report appears to have been standing for centuries, but appearances can be deceptive: this country house was completely constructed with old building materials by architect Stéphane Boens. Boens took inspiration for this project from the authentic eighteenth-century farmhouses that were common in Walloon Brabant: a long driveway leading to an entrance gate that would open out on to an inner courtyard with a main building and several outbuildings.

www.stephaneboens.be

The edges of the swimming pool have been finished in hand-worked bluestone.

The large arched windows ensure continual contact with the breathtaking natural landscape.

The bath and shower rooms and the dressing room in the swimming-pool barn.

A PERFECT SYMBIOSIS

The success of this project is to a large extent a result of the excellent relationship between the clients and the team of Jan Verlinden, a dynamic family company that in recent years has concentrated on the construction and restoration of special gardens. Both parties realised that the swimming pool, the pool house and the terraces had to be integrated into the landscape in a completely natural way, as though they had always been there.

info@ballmore.com

The pool house is constructed of reclaimed materials. The lime-rendered façade also contributes to the weathered appearance.
The swimming pool is clad with a liner. The terrace is made of bluestone tiles, some of which have been burnt or scoured.
The large box bushes are one of Jan Verlinden's specialities.

THE CHARM OF OAK-FRAMED BUILDINGS

On the English countryside, oak-framed buildings such as stables, barns and other
outbuildings make for centuries an essential part of the changing landscape.
A few years ago, Peter Pollet and Koen Bouteligier decided to breathe new
life into the old craft of building with oak timbers on the continent.
Traditional materials and craftsmanship are combined in original and timeless designs.
Only timberjointing methods are used, tightening the joints to give a uniquely strong structure.

www.heritagebuildings.be

This pool house is completely cut off as a building, because it is also used as a party room for teenagers: it has a bar, an area for showering and getting changed, and it also houses the swimming-pool machinery.
The covered terrace was the starting point for the design of the pool house: built symmetrically with the bar and with a hatch in the middle. This building is open all the way to the rafters, inside as well as outside.
The roof is clad with English Heritage tiles, specially manufactured for Heritage Buildings.

ATMOSPHERE AND AUTHENTICITY
IN AN HISTORIC FARMHOUSE

This centuries-old farmhouse in Wallonia has been transformed by Virginie
& Odile Dejaegere into a contemporary living environment.
The swimming pool, situated in one of the wings, has all the atmosphere of
the restored farmhouse and is perfectly integrated into the building.

www.interiors-dejaegere.be

A simple, serene atmosphere in the swimming-pool area. The original brick vaulting has been restored. The swimming pool is clad with glass mosaic. Surround and floor in Vietnamese bluestone. Wall lighting by Delta Light.

A CHARMING POOL HOUSE

In this report, Heritage Buildings show another beautiful project where traditional materials and craftsmanship are combined in a charming pool house with a thatched roof and a ridge in plaited erica twigs (page 33).

www.heritagebuildings.be

TIMELESS SWIMMING POOLS

De Wilde specialises in installing indoor and outdoor swimming pools in reinforced concrete with mosaic cladding. The family company also takes care of all of the finishing touches and the maintenance. The swimming pool has to fit in perfectly with the owners' lifestyle and with the look of the garden. De Wilde therefore attaches a great deal of importance to the dialogue with the client: every detail is discussed so that all of the client's wishes can be granted.

www.zwembadendewilde.be

In this project, the clay clinkers create a timeless atmosphere that fits perfectly with the architecture of this grand country house.
De Wilde also attaches a great deal of importance to perfect finishing.
The automatic roller shutters are always concealed subtly, above or below ground. The most modern disinfection technology (ionisation, ozonators and so on) ensures that the swimming pool always looks perfect.

ANGLO-AMERICAN INSPIRATION

This spacious pool house was designed by architect Olivier Dwek in an Anglo-American style that harmonises with the architecture of the house. The raised roof allows a lot of light into the pool house, the whole length of which is open, in the style of the beach huts on the East Coast of the United States. Modern touches have been subtly mixed with more classic East Coast elements. This project was created in collaboration with Frederic Luyckx and interior decorator Stéphanie Parein.

www.olivierdwek.com

The terrace around the swimming pool and the pool house is made up of polished concrete with rhythmic seams, creating the visual effect of large tiles. The grey colour of the concrete is in line with the other colours of this project: light-grey flat roof tiles, brushed-steel Starck chairs and Iroko furniture that naturally becomes grey with age.

The swimming pool is clad with grey glass mosaic.

A MONOCHROME COLOUR PALETTE
FOR A RESTORED FARM

At this restored farm, a narrow (4x12m) swimming pool has been integrated into an existing barn. Antheunis created the swimming pool, which has been clad with Chinese beige marble mosaic by Van Den Weghe. Floor in Spanish Cenia marble with an aged, bushhammered finish. The monochrome beige colour palette was provided by Couleurs Tadelakt / Odilon Creations.

www.antheunis.be   www.couleurstadelakt.com   www.vandenweghe.be

The pool area is separated from the bathroom by only a linen curtain. Floor heating has been installed throughout. Window decoration and curtains by La Campagne.

The shower room is finished with a water-resistant tadelakt technique.

IN HARMONY WITH NATURE

The design and colour of the swimming pool were of prime importance in this project because of the magnificent natural landscape. In order to achieve perfect harmony with the surroundings, a special Lapidis glass mosaic was selected: Smeralda with a Wave finish. This swimming-pool cladding gives the water a soft greenish-blue glow, which fits in perfectly with the trees and the classic villa. The stone surrounds and the terrace were built in Blu Stone (Anticato finish), also by Lapidis Mosaics.

www.lapidismosaics.com

A TIMELESS ATMOSPHERE

This garden and swimming pool were laid out only two years ago, but
already appear to have been there for decades: the greenery has already
matured and is integrated into the natural surroundings.
Following a garden design by Yves Verfaillie, Guy Moerkens was responsible for
creating the garden and terraces, which have been laid with clay clinkers.

The swimming pool has been finished with a border of specially cut bluestone.
Gunther Lambert garden furniture from Par Terre in Deurle.

NATURAL-STONE KNOW-HOW

Van den Weghe has for years been one of the most prominent
natural-stone companies in Belgium.
Director Philippe Van den Weghe has made a name for himself
as the specialist in exclusive made-to-measure work.

www.vandenweghe.be

A combination of bushhammered Carrara marble with natural lavastone from the area around Rome. Created by interior architect Lionel Jadot.

AN OASIS OF CALM

Olivier Campeert created this indoor swimming pool with a roof terrace in Overijse.
This building was designed as a long, elegant rectangle that would give a modern touch to the
classic home and a new look to the magnificent garden. The corridor between the house and the
swimming pool consists of a shower, changing room and a wine cellar, which leads to the lift.
The swimming pool has been designed to benefit from as much light as possible. The owners'
hunting trophies are displayed in an original way. This relaxing space has its own fully equipped
bar. The floor has been clad with French Massangis roche jaune natural stone and flagstones.

www.oliviercampeert.be

PERFECT HARMONY

This beautiful long-fronted farmhouse, one of architect Raymond Rombouts' unique creations, has recently been renovated by interior architect Alexis Herbosch. At the request of the owners, an extension was built and the interior of the farmhouse completely renovated. Alexis Herbosch and the owner (both keen enthusiasts of Rombouts' work) worked together to achieve harmony between the existing house and the extension. The harmony of the proportions and the use of materials resulted in a complementary whole: it looks as though the extension has always been there.

www.herbosch-vanreeth.be

Nothing was changed on the front of the farmhouse, out of respect for the original architect's creation, but also because the design studio found the clean lines of the design so breathtakingly beautiful and timeless. The original blue of the shutters provides a light-hearted accent in this simple architecture. Unusually, the swimming pool is at the front of the house.

NOOR ZAYAN

Noor Zayan is an oasis of calm and serenity in the green, rural outskirts of Marrakech. Surrounded by palms and olive trees, this spacious home with its streamlined architecture is the perfect refuge, with a view of the majestic Atlas Mountains. Architect Héléna Marczewsky created a flowing transition between the light-filled volumes and the surrounding areas with patios and large windows. This resulted in transparent views across the property. The furnishings are zen and sophisticated, with a subtle mix of contemporary furniture with eastern touches and ethnic objects.There are large terraces throughout, which invite you to take a breakfast with a panoramic view or an intimate dinner beneath the starry skies.

www.noorzayan.com

The pool house with underground spa (hammam, massage room, bathroom). Loungers by Dedon, antique Malinese chairs found in the souks of Bab Fteuh.

The hammam, with light filtered by wrought-iron moucharabias. Finish in tadelakt and Taza natural stone.

↖
In the evening, the swimming pool is illuminated by dozens of lights: a real One Thousand and One Nights atmosphere.

A HOLIDAY ATMOSPHERE

This swimming pool was created next to a contemporary
house designed by architect Reginald Schellen.

www.schellen.be

The simple, easy-to-maintain garden backs onto a wood: house, terrace, garden and woodland blend together seamlessly. The swimming pool reinforces the holiday atmosphere.

LE TEMPS DIFFERENT - GUESTHOUSE

An oasis of peace, preponderantly classic and a square farm that appeals to the imagination: the trend-setting scenario for this project for which the motivation was to aim for a spotless image. This challenging professional construction project was developed and completed by Wim Beyaert. From now on, everybody can enjoy the accomplishment: the square farm is now used as guest rooms and has been named Le Temps Différent.

www.le-temps-different.be

The choice of older materials, elegant furniture and discrete, attractive and decorative finishing in a transparent interior turn the swimming pool into an indispensable style element designed and executed by Wim Beyaert.

A MODERN TOUCH

This house was built by Vlassak-Verhulst.
Christel De Vos maintained the classic lines of the country house and restored
the swimming pool, adding a modern touch to the whole: a glass and steel cube
containing the dining room which offers a splendid view of the pool.

christeldevos1@gmail.com

A CONTEMPORARY POOL HOUSE

Architect Pascal van der Kelen created a new pool house and a contemporary swimming pool from the terrace by the long side of a renovated house. The bottom part of the glass section consists of three windows that slide independently of each other and can be arranged in different positions.

www.pascalvanderkelen.com

A COSMOPOLITAN ATMOSPHERE

A big-city, cosmopolitan atmosphere in green surroundings on the edge
of Brussels, yet still close to the city centre: this private residence, created
by architect Marc Corbiau, offers the best of both worlds.
Raoul Cavadias, a Belgian designer with Greek roots who was born in Africa
and grew up in Switzerland, took care of the interior design of this distinctive
city villa which radiates a sense of space, serenity and sophistication.

www.raoul-cavadias.com

A roughly cut Iranian red travertine was selected for around the swimming pool and as wall panelling.

The swimming pool itself has been clad with cobalt-blue Bisazza mosaic.

Walls and ceilings in pale-green acoustic plaster.

Stairs in perforated sheet steel with rust-coloured paint.

The curving overflow area lengthens the pillars by providing a reflection in the water. The shades and atmosphere of this swimming pool were inspired by Villa Majorelle in Marrakech.

A COUNTRY HOUSE NEAR BRUSSELS

This country house, situated in the green outskirts of Brussels, was built in the 1920s and has recently been renovated for the second time. The renovation work took almost a year and was carried out according to the owners' comfort wishes: a new, larger swimming pool was installed to replace the old one and a sports pavilion was added. The garden was completely redesigned.

www.esthergutmer.be

The surroundings of the country house were redesigned by landscape architect Yves Verfaillie.
A swimming pool with chiselled bluestone surround.
Terrace in bushhammered bluestone.

A SPLENDID 180° PANORAMA

This house "with its feet in the water" in the parkland of Saint-Tropez boasts magnificent views, but had been neglected for many years. Esther Gutmer created a completely new structure, dividing the house into three living spaces, with all rooms enjoying a sea view. The outside areas and the garden were redesigned and offer a splendid 180° panorama.

www.esthergutmer.be

A view of the entrance
to this holiday home.

SERENITY AND MINIMALISM

Serenity and minimalism in this swimming pool room designed by 'Aksent.
Gong daybed by Promemoria.

www.aksent-gent.be

BEAUTIFUL REFLECTIONS

Architect Pascal van der Kelen has created an outdoor swimming pool in the inner courtyard
of his private house. The new inner courtyard is oriented to the south-west. A system of
windows and enamelled glass reflects the green surroundings. The water surface mirrors
the buildings and the sky and provides right-angled reflections of the new building.

www.pascalvanderkelen.com

CONTEMPORARY FEEL

This contemporary house, built by architect Librecht in the 1970s, was thoroughly transformed by the Brussels design office Instore. The garden was designed by Dominique Eeman. The original painted-brick walls have been cemented. An outdoor swimming pool and a pool house have been added by the new owners.

www.instore.be   www.eeman.net

Various polished concrete terraces were placed around the swimming pool in a hammered anti-slip finish with insets of tropical ipé wood. The edge of the swimming pool is finished in lacquered steel. The grey lining of the swimming pool (the same grey cement colour as the exterior walls) gives the water a subdued blue-grey colour.
Chaises longues and garden chairs by G. Belotti from the 'Outdoor' collection by Alias.

EPISCOPAL INSPIRATION

This residence for a family with three growing children was built by
architect Bernard De Clerck in a classic eighteenth-century style:
he drew his inspiration from a bishop's country seat near Bruges, which dates back to 1750.
The quality of the light, the creation of perspectives and the optimal
orientation of the rooms were important in the design of this house.
All the spaces are arranged around an inner courtyard, which means that the
occupants can enjoy the sunlight in different rooms for most of the day.

info@bernarddeclerck.be

The indoor horizon swimming pool. Flooring in rust-coloured, rough lava rock.

The relaxation area by the swimming pool. The glass door leads to the fitness room above the swimming pool.

THE CONTEMPORARY RENOVATION
OF AN AUTHENTIC FAMILY HOME

This country house, which was furnished around
ten years ago by the late Jean de Meulder,
has recently been redesigned by Gilles de Meulemeester.
He also added a new wing in the original spirit of the house. The floor
around the swimming pool is clad with grey acid-washed stone.

www.ebony-interiors.com

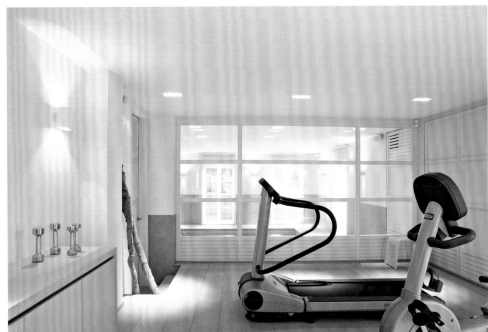

The fitness room looks out over the swimming pool.

The hammam was created in Sicis mosaic. The open shower is clad in the same stone as the swimming pool.

WELLNESS IN A STATELY COUNTRY VILLA

This renovation project in the green environs around Antwerp was entrusted
to Sphere Concepts from Schilde. They contacted architect Gerd Van Zundert
(AID-Architecten) to adapt the outer walls and to bring these into the correct
proportions, after Sphere Concepts had designed the interior layout.
The previous layout of the villa was dated, and Sphere Concepts replaced this
with an interior that radiates charm, and in particular peace and quiet.

www.sphereconcepts.be

The indoor swimming pool was faced in white mosaic and edged with light fawn coloured natural stone. Bamboo shutters were painted white.

The glazed sauna, double shower and jacuzzi were cobble-clad. The LED lighting can be adjusted to the mood.

A ROMANTIC COUNTRY HOUSE

In a green parkland municipality to the north of Antwerp, Costermans built a timeless country house adjacent to a natural pond and surrounded by lovely trees. For the exterior only natural and warm materials were used, old 'paepesteen' (hand-made bricks) in cross-bond, oak and wrought-iron windows, gradated brownish-red little pan tiles and a cosy covered terrace under a thatched roof. The atmosphere in the residence is airy and warm, and shirks excess. This country house has an outdoor and an indoor pool.

www.costermans-projecten.be

The rear of the building looks out over a large natural pond, where a little romantically arched hardwood bridge gives access to an island with wooden decking. The swimming pool is finished in grey pebbles, which provide for a natural azure-blue colour. The rear side of the swimming pool overflow runs over on the pond side, such as to give an extra feeling of freedom whilst you are swimming. The cosy terraces are connected to all the living spaces in this residence, and on warm days and in the evenings it is pleasant to sit on the covered terrace near the kitchen.

Next to the utility room and giving directly onto the covered terrace, we find the indoor swimming pool with Turkish bath and sauna. The swimming pool is finished in white pebbles, combined with Murano glass mosaic by the brand Sicis, which has also been used for the Turkish bath. The ergonomic benches ensure enjoyable comfort.

A SYMBIOSIS WITH NATURE

On a plot of five hectares in the heart of the Lasnoise countryside, this detached house has been completely renovated by the architects Sébastien and Michel Losseau, of the SA A.D.M. firm. Out of a desire to recreate an environment in symbiosis with nature, the owners have kept the existing equestrian activity and have embellished the property with numerous man-made lakes and fountains.

www.loupandco.com

A TIMELESS GARDEN IN AN EXCEPTIONAL SETTING

Jan Joris (Landscape Gardening) was asked to integrate the unspoilt scenery and the various buildings into a single whole with numerous vistas and different atmospheres. The contrasts of light/shadow, open/closed, rigid/loose and high/low, respect for the existing nature and the four seasons are recurring themes in all the designs worked out by Jan Joris Tuinarchitectuur. The close collaboration between the owner, villa contractor Frank Missotten and the team of Jan Joris resulted in this project.

www.janjoristuinen.be

ENGLISH INSPIRATION

Ilse De Meulemeester Interieur created this residence in close cooperation with villa builder
Elbeko from Zele and the architects' firm of engineer and architect Bart François in Ghent.
The assignment seemed simple: to design a timeless country house with the
historical impact of a traditional English cottage, which would be a beacon
of peace and quiet and a place with a permanent holiday feel to it.

www.bartfrancois.be   www.ilsedemeulemeester.be

In the middle is the overflow swimming pool, surrounded by the orangery, living area, entrance hall, garages and covered terrace.

A DESIGNER'S HOME IN CAPE TOWN

Project architects Richard Townsend and Stefan Antoni used a 'sea-farm' inspiration
to create a holiday house for a small family in Cape Town (South Africa).
The house was to have a feature double volume space with very simple clean
lines and needed to flow seamlessly between interior and exterior.
The clients, being in the design world, were particularly sensitive to colour and were very
much involved in choosing the materials used in both the interior and exterior of the home.

www.saota.com

The balau timber and dark travertine terrace with balau timber pergola and cantilevered seat. All planting is indigenous.

↖
A detail of the stone-clad
water-feature, gently
falling into the rim-flow
pool. The pool is lined
with blue-grey mosaics.

LOTS OF SPACE

This house was designed by the Brussels architect Fabien Van Tomme. The garden and surroundings are by Buro Groen. All of the exterior walls have been plastered. Windows with stainless-steel frames and lots of space. Wooden terraces.

www.fabienvantomme.be　　www.obumex.be　　www.burogroen.be

A long wall runs alongside the swimming pool, allowing swimmers a low glimpse of the garden and clearly separating the terrace and swimming pool from the garden to create an outdoor room.

A CHALET IN THE FRENCH ALPS

This mountain chalet is set amidst picturesque scenery in the French
Alps. The traditional architecture was reinterpreted
so that the magnificent views could be enjoyed to best effect, whilst the
interior is a luxurious mixture of style, comfort and a modern lifestyle.
The design team of Moulder, Laxer + Salter of F3 Architects in London worked together
with Base Contracts and local professionals in order to complete this
extraordinary residence and have it ready for immediate occupation.

www.f3architects.co.uk   www.basecontracts.com

A BEAUTIFUL MOUNTAIN VIEW

This elegant apartment, located in a building of recent construction
in the centre of Crans-Montana, was designed and built entirely by
interior architect Marina Wenger and her Version M team.
It boasts a beautiful mountain view.

www.versionm.com

The ceiling with indirect lighting creates a considerable feeling of spaciousness.

A LUMINOUS MINIMALISM

Olivier Michel, the founder and driving force behind Upptown, is one of the most talked-about project developers of recent years. In a very desirable area of Ukkel (Brussels region), he discovered a group of dilapidated warehouses and garages, which he soon transformed into a residential project with four ultramodern lofts. The intention was to sell all four properties, but Michel and his wife were so enthusiastic about this project that they joined together two of the lofts for themselves to create one large property of over 600m², with its own garden, a swimming pool and two patio areas. The construction work was entrusted to architect Bruno Corbisier.

The swimming pool is outside, but the large sheets of glass ensure that it enters into a close interaction with the interior.

The shower cubicle, lined with black mosaic tiles, is concealed behind a glass wall with a black enamel finish.

EIGHTEENTH-CENTURY INSPIRATION FOR A COUNTRY MANOR

Architect Bernard De Clerck designed a country manor in a traditional style for a young family that enjoys an informal way of life and being in close contact with nature: quiet, calming and sophisticated. The eighteenth century was an important source of inspiration for this project. Bernard De Clerck created the whole house: outside as well as inside. His clients gave him a great deal of support with this, as did the capable specialists who carried out his designs to the smallest detail. The swimming house emanates peace and serenity. Italy, and Tuscany in particular, is a recurrent theme of inspiration for colours and textures.

info@bernarddeclerck.be

The fitness room in the vaulted cellars has subtle illumination. The floor is laid with
old terracotta tiles. Behind the wooden screen is a shower room.

CASA NERO

Casa Nero refers to the name of the interior design agency of the owners (Casa Vero) and to the black brick volume that makes up their home, designed by BBSC-Architects. Closed on the roadside (strengthened by the patio where the public area switches to the private area) but completely open towards the broad meadow landscape at the back, which makes contact with nature optimal.

www.casavero.be

AN ARCHITECTURAL REFLEX TO THE SEA

Located on top of a promontory, this villa was completely restructured "feet in the
water" style, and enlarged by GEF Réalisations, the office for interior design.
Transparency, lightness and luminosity were the keywords in this project.
The interior design, which is extended outdoors and in the garden,
was subtly designed by landscape designer Loup & Co.,
who extends the architectural reflex to the sea.

www.loupandco.com

Wood, natural stone
and a coloured canopy
animate the pool area.

AN ICON OF CONTEMPORARY AESTHETICS

An architect-designed bungalow from 1959 was spectacularly transformed into an icon of contemporary minimalist aesthetics and exclusive modern-day living comfort by Van Aken Architects of Eindhoven. Zeth Interior design & construction (Rob Zeelen) was responsible for the design of this unique home.

www.vanakenarchitecten.nl   www.zeth.nl

A UNIQUE GARDEN

This project by Jan Joris Landscaping, came about together with the client
and in close consultation with architect Frank Van Laere and designer / artist
Thierry Lejeune: a unique, contemporary garden in a beautiful setting.
Two major lines of sight were used for the work inside the house.
Along one axis this was reinforced by a long narrow pond (in
aluminium and a path with artwork on the other side).
Another axis was subtly drawn from the gate, the door to the whole rear.

www.janjoristuinen.be

VIEW OF THE LAKE

This garden by Joost Valgaeren & co, at a modern house designed by the architect Daniël Willekens, looks out over an old sand dredging site in the Kempen. Two large terraces constitute the main areas in the garden. The particular floor plan creates a feeling of security on the terrace. Different axes, accented by grasses, draw the eye to the terrace on the waterside and the old sand dredging site. The keynotes of this project were the sleek, timeless architecture of the house, the white plaster facade, the aluminium and stainless steel details, the sober choice of materials in the garden ... and the majestic view of the lake. Jeroen Martens (Mira Verde) decorated the terrace with outdoor furniture from Fuer a Dentro, in combination with Tuuci parasols, Gooooo design vases and the decorative Cores da Terra apples. As the basic colour he opted for white (modern, timeless, sober and summery) with a lime green accent.

www.miraverde.be   www.joostvalgaeren.be

UNDER THE MEDITERRANEAN SUN

This property is located in Ste Maxime (Southern France). It enjoys double views: sea / mountains. A new approach to the traditional architecture of the Mediterranean Sea makes for a resolutely contemporary style here. Décoration Cartier, a study bureau and showroom for contemporary furniture in Lyon, designed an innovative contemporary living environment in dialogue with the customer, the focus being on modernity and comfort. The external architecture is reflected by the several terraces which correspond to the double exposure: sea / mountains. The landscape architecture here was designed in function of the dialogue between the wild Mediterranean nature and the more subdued contemporary living spaces. Garden furniture by Dedon and a Porro dining table, sofas and armchairs by Gandia Blasco. The terrace is made of ipe.

www.decorationcartier.com

MODERN, SLEEK AND WHITE

Before the design for this pool house was finalised, BoGarden had made several drafts. In the early phases the pool house was intended to be built in hardwood, but as a result of many dialogues with the customer and in consultation with garden architect Veerle Smet a modern, sleek, white pool house was chosen. The pool house consists of a timber frame modular housing system with white roughcast plastering on it. Aluminium windows with minimal window profiles were provided. For the terrace roof, a floating awning was chosen, without a supporting pole, to allow a maximum view of the garden.

www.bogarden.be   www.hvo.be   www.veerlesmet.be   www.philippedewilde.be

THE RENOVATION OF AN EXCLUSIVE DREAM HOME

Project developer and entrepreneur Alexander Cambron creates about
three top-quality residential projects a year. These "prêt-à-habiter" homes
focus entirely on the wishes and requirements of the new owners.
In this project, Alexander Cambron shows the health and relaxation space with
indoor swimming pool, gym, hammam and jacuzzi in an exclusive dream home.
The swimming pool can be raised to turn the space into a reception area. The
large sliding doors open onto the sun deck and fill this space with light.

www.alexandershouses.com

THE ART OF LIVING ON THE CÔTE D'AZUR

Commissioned by a property developer, RR interior Concepts took this newly built villa in Saint-Tropez completely in hand. In this project Christel De Vos concentrated entirely on the complete furnishing and finishing. Both for outside and inside the furniture selected came from Flexform, B&B Italia, Minotti, Maxalto,…The object was to create a pleasant environment where the surroundings and the finished interior form a single united whole. Fresh colours, in combination with a black contrast, show a controlled vision. This is an example of the art of living outside the Belgian frontiers; a challenge from which RR Interior Concepts certainly did not shrink.

www.rrinterieur.be   christeldevos1@gmail.com

SPACE AND LIGHT IN HARMONY

A young couple with three children built this luxurious house, together with Crepain Binst architectural studio. They called upon the services of 'aksent for the complete interior design. It was important that the clean, modern lines of the apartment should not become too chilly and cold. Stefan Paeleman from 'Aksent took a contemporary approach that differs significantly from the normal designer look. The words 'past' and 'future' were important themes here.

www.aksent-gent.be

The basement houses the relaxation space with a hammam, whirlpool bath, sauna, shower and swimming pool. The hammam and whirlpool bath are lined with marble mosaic. Floor in combe brune stone. The teakwood walls create a feeling of warmth. Recliners by Piet Boon. The swimming pool has been lined with black pebbles.

TRENDSETTER IN EXCLUSIVE TILES

The successful combination of colour and proportions ensures a sense
of calm and balance in this health and relaxation space.
The green and pale-grey glass mosaic has been combined with a ceramic tile
(imitation Pietra Piasentina marble) and a surround in Agrippa.

www.devostegelbedrijf.be

VIRTUOSITY IN COLOUR

In this Costermans project, a spa and swimming pool lie behind a plain wrought-iron door. The blue-tinted Moroccan zelliges create a Mediterranean atmosphere.

www.costermans-projecten.be

AN AGE-OLD PATINA

Although the country house in this report was constructed only recently, it seems to have a patina of great age. This is not only the result of the consistent use of weathered and reclaimed materials on the exterior, the interior also has a timeless, historic atmosphere. Dankers Decor, who have a royal warrant and are one of the most renowned Belgian decorating companies, created a harmony of colours throughout the whole house, using Arte Constructo's lime paints, coloured with natural pigments: an "à la carte" solution for this beautiful house.

www.arteconstructo.be   www.dankers.be

Dankers Decor finished the walls around the swimming pool in a lime plaster.

RURAL CHARM WITH A TOUCH OF STATELINESS

In these magnificent surroundings, Vlassak Verhulst has created a charming home in the so-called "demesne" style. The house and its lands radiate a delightful charm and relaxed atmosphere. It has all the ingredients needed to make this residence a real home where people can come and relax completely.

www.vlassakverhulst.be

The garden runs seamlessly into the landscape behind.

↖
The garden and terrace are
the work of 't Huis van
Oordeghem. A Saler sofa,
an Ensombra parasol and
Sahara pots, all from Gandia
Blasco. The 1966 loungers
are from B&B Italia.

HAUTE COUTURE IN SWIMMING POOL DESIGN

In this report Bob Monteyne shows an outdoor swimming pool recently provided for a
house designed by architect Stéphane Boens, as well as an indoor swimming pool.

www.bobmonteyne.be

AN OASIS OF PEACE

When this villa was being converted, the owners contacted Heritage Buildings to build a pool house next to the swimming pool. This pool house was to serve not only for the technical facilities for the swimming pool (including changing room and shower), but the wish list also included a large, covered terrace. The owners like to spend time with their family and friends here, in the middle of the garden. For Heritage Buildings the main challenge was to create a lovely, charming whole that fulfilled all the desiderata, separate from the main building. So they opted for a tiled roof, to highlight the contrast with the main building. With their design, Heritage Buildings created a very private area around the swimming pool, but one where it is still possible to enjoy the splendid view of the garden.

www.heritagebuildings.be

As time goes by the planks take on the same silver-grey patina as the oak structure without any maintenance. Behind the covered terrace lies a complete pool house, including changing area, shower and technical facilities.

A SUBTLE HOLIDAY FEELING

In this report, landscape and garden architect Dominique Eeman demonstrates his creativity and virtuosity. For both holiday homes, he has succeeded in creating a subtle holiday feeling using a balanced mix of evergreen shrubs, grasses, weathered and natural materials (natural stone, wood), with a swimming pool and a swimming pond that are perfectly integrated into the surroundings.

www.eeman.net

The garden furniture was designed by Piet Boon.

The overspill
swimming pool is
approximately 14
meters in length
and is a Nobelpool
creation.

The owners of this 1930s house did not want a real swimming pool due to environmental concerns. So they opted in favour of a swimming pond, consisting of a bath that is worked with a black basalt stone, in which the water is filtered through a separate marsh filter that lies behind the swimming section but also in line with the front door. This pond can also be heated (a project by Tuinteam bvba, Veurne). Bluestone edging and narrow pathways in small clay paving stones set in a coursed pattern (Vande Moortel, "Ancienne Belgique"). To enhance the relaxed atmosphere, the terrace was laid with padauk wood, combined with garden furniture from Piet Boon. Austere plants including Buxus, roses, lime trees, etc. The pool house was created by Gino Van Der Jeught (Outside Wood Works).

OUTDOOR LUXURY

Landscape architect Xavier Loup and architect/decorator Coralie Michiels complement each other perfectly in their company Loup & Co with offices in Paris and Arquennes. This article introduces a new show garden at Arquennes. In the show garden Loup & Co has unveiled a wide range of 'outdoor luxury': terraces, designer furniture, patios, garden lighting, special ornaments and much more besides. The company is a distributor of exclusive such as Kettal, Roda, Domani, Royal Botania, Moroso, Kartell, Tekna and Atelier Vierkant and also markets a series of 'limited editions' and pots with the Loup & Co signature. Versatility is unquestionably the key success factor of Loup & Co: the company coordinates the total garden experience from A to Z, including architect, designer, decorator, engineer and supplier. All these key players are available through one-stop shopping at Loup & Co.

www.loupandco.com

The swimming pool has been designed like a basin. A combination of slate and blue hard stone from Hainaut provides an austere yet serene setting. Three containers of Equisetum arvensis and Juncus tenageia were planted in a separate zone. This sun terrace has been demarcated with hedges in Taxus baccata, young Ficus carrica and pots made of compressed clay.

The show garden of Loup & Co covers more than 5000 m² and is located south of Brussels on the motorway to Paris. The photograph shows a view from the office, with a decorative plant basin at the swimming pool.

ARCHITECTURE & NATURE, AN EXCITING COMBINATION

This swimming pool was designed by architect Hans Verstuyft as a combination of a walk-below and walk-above system. This made it possible to deal with the height difference in the garden. The terrace is lower than the water level, creating a more intimate feeling. The pool house was created as a wooden, ageing shed. On the elevated floor there is a sauna and relaxation area. The house, swimming pool and pool house have been embedded independently of each other, but still remain interconnected.

www.hansverstuyftarchitecten.be

A MASTER OF SPACES

Van den Weghe (The Stone Company) has realized the natural stone works
in this jacuzzi and relaxation corner of the Ommerstein Castle.
The jacuzzi is built to accomodate six seated persons and is clad in Bisazza
mosaic. The rear wall is in sandstone coloured to harmonize with natural
stone. Built-in Kreon spotlights create the right atmosphere.

www.vandenweghe.be

A view of the relaxation corner. Cushions in Pierre Frey fabrics (by Jozef Reynaerts). The entrance to the shower and sauna is set at an angle.
This gives it a greater volume that is in proportion with the architecture of the vaulted cellar.
Stairs and floor are all by Van den Weghe with a bush-hammered finish.

TRENDSETTING

This project is by BoGarden, a trendsetting company in
modern outbuildings, pool houses, car ports, etc.

www.bogarden.be

A SURPRISING PLAY OF LIGHT

This pool area is covered with bush-hammered bluestone (floor and pillars). The indirect light ensures a surprising play of light. Next to the swimming pool there is also a hammam, covered with mosaics.

www.descamps.be

OUTDOOR LIVING

These two BoGarden projects invite the home owners and their
guests to live outdoors: a perfectly integrated swimming pool,
large terraces, a pool house with dining and kitchen area,...

www.bogarden.be

The pool house with the thatched roof has been designed and realized by BoGarden.

AN OVERFLOW POOL WITH BEAUTIFUL RIVER VIEWS

This «Bain du Nord» swimming pool with a polyester coating
has been created by Philippe De Wilde.
Terraces in padauk by Timbertech-Cornilly.
The pool house is a BoGarden creation.

www.philippedewilde.be   www.bogarden.be

AN OASIS OF SPACE

As with all of its other projects, the Schellen architectural studio created
both the architecture and the interior of this contemporary home.
Linda Coart was responsible for the functional and clean design,
which extends seamlessly from outside to inside.

www.schellen.be

On the garden side of the house, large glass sections ensure a perfect connection between inside and outside. The interplay of extensive sheets of glass, freestanding columns, horizontal canopies and vertical sections is a trademark of architect Reginald Schellen. The garden, with its clean lines, is by Tom Caes.

The quartz-zinc makes another appearance as a material for the pool house (created by Ilse Plancke).

A VERY RELAXING POOL HOUSE

This pool house has been created next to an outdoor
swimming pool by architect Bernard De Clerck.
The pool house is a very relaxing space, with a sauna,
hammam, jacuzzi, fitness and relaxation centre.

info@bernarddeclerck.be

ENDLESS VIEWS

Nothing remains of the original appearance of these four houses from the 1950s which were combined into a contemporary and luxurious single-family home. The restructuring of its various levels and functionality revolved around a patio which now lets natural light into the heart of the house. With taste and determination, the owner allowed Oliver and Hélène Lempereur to go to the end with their ideas.

www.olivierlempereur.com

AN OASIS OF PEACE AND RELAXATION

Architect Stéphane Boens created a wellness environment in a stately
home in the green surroundings of Antwerp: indoor swimming pool,
hammam, luxurious bathrooms, a bar and a wine cellar.
In close consultation with Dominique Desimpel (Tegels Dominique Desimpel) a
harmonious blend of exclusive, warm varieties of natural stone was chosen here.

www.stephaneboens.be   www.tegelsdesimpel.be

The hammam was covered in Palon stone.

THE PERFECT WELLNESS EXPERIENCE
IN A STATELY HOME

Themenos designed the indoor swimming pool in this stately home.
The natural stonework was carried out by Van den Weghe (The Stone Company).

www.themenos.be   www.vandenweghe.be

The floors around the swimming pool are covered in Gris Sau natural stone with a burnished finish and thereby received a perfect anti-slip treatment.

The edge of the swimming pool has the same finishing as the floor but seems darker because it is under water. The bath itself is covered with mosaics from Antheunis.

A WOODED GARDEN FULL OF CONTRAST

This house is situated in an extensive wooded landscape, made up of oaks, birches, pine trees and rhododendrons, with undergrowth consisting mainly of marram grass. The site has very clear contours, with hilly ridges, slopes and ponds. Jan Joris landscaping consultancy from Brasschaat was asked to reshape this unspoilt natural area and the house to create a harmonious whole. The natural wood forms the backdrop; the people and their living environment are all part of the surrounding nature. The natural ridges and pond determined the location and the levels of the various buildings. Wherever you are – inside or outside – you are aware of the contrast between garden and nature.

www.janjoris.be

The garden is an oasis in the wood. The yew and Prunus provide security and create a sense of depth when seen from the house. These green shapes do not only give a distinctive look to the façade of the house, but also create balance with the wooded landscape.

The woodland vegetation of marram grass grows right up to the windows of the swimming pool.

HARMONY BETWEEN A GARDEN AND THE LANDSCAPE
NEAR THE FLEMISH ARDENNES

This garden is situated around an 18th-century farmhouse complex in the immediate surroundings of the Flemish Ardennes. Garden designer Vincent Verlinden incorporated this magnificent landscape into his design, integrating the panoramic views within the garden. The garden has gradually gained its definitive shape over the years and through successive seasons, always in close consultation with the owners. Sometimes small changes have been made, sometimes more dramatic ones. In spite of the not insubstantial size of the grounds, this garden is very easy to maintain: there are no flower borders or other labour-intensive features. Three or so pruning sessions a year are sufficient.

The terrace garden around the swimming pool has partial shade from the old holly hedge. On the other side is a view of the natural pond and the orchard beyond.

An old holly hedge has been restored to its former glory and sculpted into a new shape. The low yew hedge accentuates the lines of the swimming pool. Contrasts between relaxed and formal shapes can be seen throughout almost the whole garden.

↖
The wooden planks run through from the covered area to the space around the swimming pool, connecting the garden with the house.

Calm and simplicity, harmonious use of materials and a well-balanced planting scheme. The wooden outer gate has been replaced by a hinged metal window construction, so that contact with the inner courtyard is possible. The wooden gate has been retained on the courtyard side so as to preserve the special character of this space.

ARCHITECTURAL AND SCULPTURAL

The house in this report was built in 1930, as a residence and guest quarters
for the son of Villers castle, in the green countryside outside Antwerp.
In 1990 the estate was bought and renovated by the current owners.
With the exception of the old trees, the garden has been completely redesigned
and replanted by Piet Gysel and Marc Moris (Groep Moris).
The result is a garden very much inspired by architecture and
sculpture, created in close collaboration with the owners.

www.groepmoris.eu

The swimming pool is
surrounded by box, yew, beech
and standing hornbeam.

LE PAQUEBOT: A MODERNIST MASTERPIECE
BY MARCEL LEBORGNE

In 1929 the architect Marcel Leborgne designed the Villa Diricks for the then CEO of Forges de Clabecq: a mater in the art of living who wanted to find the allure and atmosphere in his own home of the chic international hotels he often visited. This "city palace" was greatly inspired by Le Corbusier at the front; at the rear this villa lives up to its nickname "Le Paquebot" (the passenger ship). Almost eighty years after the creation the property developer Alexander Cambron and his team realised a remarkable rehabilitation of this unique example of modernist heritage. The original architecture of the listed and reputed masterpiece naturally was respected completely but at the same time thoroughly redeveloped.

www.alexandershouses.com

BALINESE INSPIRATION

The interior decorator Fabienne Dupont was given carte blanche for the renovation of this indoor swimming pool: together with the interior architect Vincent Bruyninckx and her loyal staff she had full rein in this project. The garden around was already planted with bamboo and this luxuriant, exotic décor was the inspiration for the swimming pool: a holiday feel in Balinese style, zen and restful to give some sun during the long winter days. Fabienne chose LED and neon lighting that was designed to create a warm whole. Everything is dark: black beams, large black paving stones in and around the swimming pool that give the water a beautiful dark green colour.

www.alexandershouses.com   www.fabathome.be

There are fake and real doors around made from steel frames that sometimes serve as decoration, sometimes as actual doors to close off the shower, hamam, dressing room and rest area. These frames were filled with bamboo sticks in the same colour as the wall.

The pool was made larger by integrating stairs with a blower and a Jacuzzi. The stairs are used like a seat. The heating is concealed in a band with black stones. The dehumidifier is concealed behind the bamboo doors.

A SUCCESSFUL START

This was Alexander Cambron's first project: the beginning
of a career full of exciting, exclusive homes.
This existing, small villa was transformed into a living
environment with a lot of space and a sea of light.
The house was extended with a huge wooden orangery, the existing outside walls remained
intact, with new window openings as a passage between the two living rooms.

www.alexandershouses.com

A swimming pool was installed in the garden, covered with grey concrete and bluestone edging stones. There are lots of concealed nooks in the garden: a sauna in the garden shed, a horse stable, etc.

FASCINATING BLEND OF TRADITION AND MODERNITY

Where once a neglected vegetable patch grew rampant, architect Gilles Pellerin
has created an exceptional living space in which traditional Mediterranean
architecture is blended harmoniously with contemporary elements. The location
is unique: situated on a rock halfway up a hill, with the bay of Cannes
as the décor and breathtaking views all the way from Saint-Tropez to Italy.

www.collection-privee.com

Pairs of cypresses give rhythm
to the different levels.

The monochrome beige
colours of the façades, the
terraces and the edging stones
of the swimming pool exude
soberness and serenity.

PAYING TRIBUTE TO A RICH ARCHITECTURAL HISTORY

In this project, as in the previous report, Vlassak-Verhulst reveal their fondness for the rustic style of architecture, created according to traditional methods and owing a great deal to our rich history of construction.
The harmony of house and garden is a central feature of this project as well: this country house has been completely integrated into its beautiful natural surroundings.

www.vlassakverhulst.be

A pool house in typical Kempen style with its covered terrace and old oak supports.
Virginia creeper grows around the canopy.

RUSTIC INSPIRATION

This countryside villa was designed by the Demyttenaere
architectural studio from Knokke.
The side wall to the left of the house is covered
with wisteria and climbing hydrangea.

www.myth.be

The covered terrace with the pool house, and a completely rebuilt space to the right of it, which now contains the kitchen and dining area. The large, new glass doors in the central section lend a new elegance to this side of the house.

INSPIRED BY THE ENGLISH COUNTRYSIDE

Home Development Company built this English inspired villa in the green belt around Antwerp. Warm, natural materials were chosen for the exterior, perfectly in harmony with the green surroundings.

www.homedc.be   www.janjoris.com

The swimming pool (8m x 4m) has an underflow system to give extra emphasis to the board in massive Belgian bluestone.
Stepping stones in old Dutch clay paving stones. The outside wall was built with old Bruges moef stones.

A HOUSE IN THE DUNES

This house was designed by Pieter Popeye (PVL Architects) for a retired married couple that commutes between warmer climes and the Flemish coast. It is an easy-to-maintain pied-à-terre that can be enjoyed throughout one's life, magnificently situated near dunes. The stunning views determine the dimensions, orientation and layout of the house. It is clear that the design is built from the inside out: a monumental rectangular volume in which some openings and repositionings generate interesting indoor and outdoor spaces, closed and open as necessary.

www.pvlarchitecten.be

On the ground floor along with a garage and cellars for technical systems, there is a beautiful pool area with matching changing room, bathroom and guest bedroom. The paving, bluestone blocks fitted groutlessly, was extended all the way from the street-side driveway to the terrace along the rear of the house. The high windows with sunken sills give the impression that the interior and exterior spaces flow seamlessly into one another.

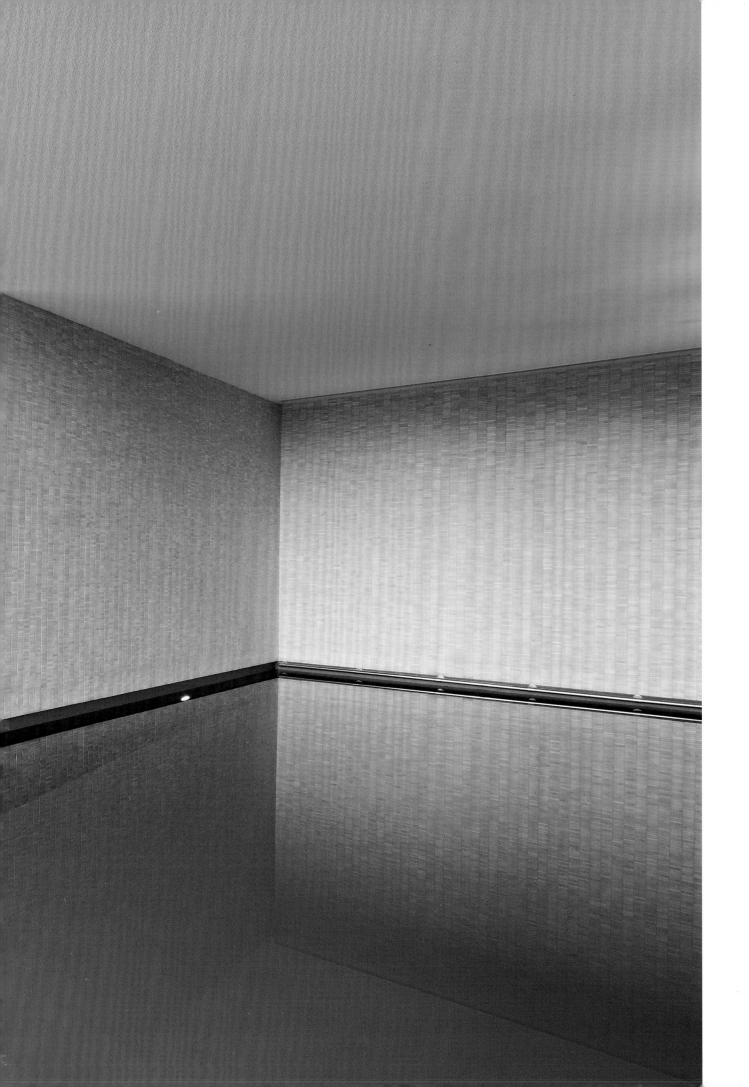

PEACE AND QUIET

This haven of peace and quiet was created near Kortrijk and nestles in a green oasis.
The existing house was completely redesigned by interior architect Steven
Compernol in collaboration with architect Rudy Vandeputte. The synergy between
interior and exterior was the starting point for this conversion. Both the design
and materials used are the result of this interaction. The result is a interplay of
closed volumes with surprising openings and views to the garden all around.

www.archi2.be

The swimming pool is located in the axis of the dining room and the master bedroom.

↖
The pool house has the same
details as the tower.

A REAL METAMORPHOSIS

A new wing was added to the existing L-shaped house, built around the existing sunken terrace. It was conceived as a glass box, partly with windows, partly white enamelled glass. The challenge was to create a canopy that would only be 15mm thick. A sunken swimming pool with its own terraces was built in line with the new wing. The existing buildings were completely refurbished. A first floor was added over part of the original building with a roof clad in copper. Also the entire interior design of the building was done by the Aurora-projects company, in line with the plans created by the architect Pascal van der Kelen.

www.pascalvanderkelen.com   www.pascalvanderkelencollection.com

The challenge for the architect was to create a glass space with a canopy only 15mm thick. All walls are finished in white enamelled glass. The beautiful existing sunken terrace was renovated. The new U-shaped configuration of the building emphasizes the deliberate rectangle of the terrace.

A HOLIDAY FEELING IN A CONTEMPORARY SETTING

The principals, both very active people in their 40s with a busy agenda, wanted to convert the villa they had bought and which lies in thickly wooded surroundings into a place where coming home means living in another world, in which there is room for professional and domestic activities and in which a holiday feeling can never be far away either. There was also a request to maximise the contact with the garden and to build a covered, outdoor space in the garden. The building was completely stripped.

www.steinvanrossem.be

Outdoor view towards the bedroom. The sleeping area forms a covered place of rest with the window open.
The ceiling, wall and floor frame the view over the garden by the outdoor woodwork, free from disturbing elements such as window frames, curtains and sunblinds. This optimises the observation towards the garden, which not only brings the garden indoors; life indoors is also seen as a showcase from the outside.

↖
The swimming pool, with
the same ceramic tiles, and
the connected outdoor salon
"Eco".

AN OASIS OF CALM

This house, designed by architect Pascal Bilquin, shelters behind a fully closed front outer wall in the middle of the greenery of Laarne. All the rooms are bathed in light behind the front outer wall and offer a view over the beautiful garden and patio. Minus designed a sober interior with only three tints throughout the house: the black of the slates, the matt white of the whitewashed walls and the warm fervour of natural oak. Enter an oasis of rest...

www.minus.be

The whiteness of the swimming pool breathes tranquillity. The green of the garden plays a prominent role.

THE LUXURY OF SPACE

Space is a luxury…
…and in this magnificent creation by Marc Corbiau, the spaces are nothing short of majestic.
Ensemble & Associés have recreated the fittings, finishes and atmosphere of
this home in order to best meet the requirements of its new owners.
Simple materials and colours, flowing lines and efficient
organisation are all hallmarks of the design.

www.ensembleetassocies.be

INTERIOR/EXTERIOR

In a house whose lines were decided by architect Bruno Moinard (an interior designer from Paris), Obumex architect Vangroenweghe has achieved a fitting interior. The interaction between interior and exterior (the garden with its inviting swimming pool) is very important in this project.

www.obumex.be

A TIMELESS SUMMER HOUSE

Architect Frank Van Laere has restored an ancient shed into a
timeless summer house with outdoor swimming pool.
The garden was designed by Ludo Dierckx.

www.ludodierckx.be

SEAMLESSLY INTEGRATED

These swimming pools created by De Wilde run seamlessly into the landscape behind.

www.zwembadendewilde.be

THE BEAUTY OF BELGIAN BLUESTONE

The floor around this swimming pool has been clad with Belgian bluestone from Saillart.

www.saillart.be

This swimming pool was designed by architect Stéphane Boens.

PUBLISHER
BETA-PLUS publishing
www.betaplus.com

PHOTOGRAPHY
Jo Pauwels

DESIGN
Polydem – Nathalie Binart

ISBN : 978-90-8944-120-1

Coordination production printing and binding :
www.belvedere.nl - André Kloppenberg
Printing and binding: Printer Trento, Italy